Antarmukhi

Antarmukhi

A novel method of meditation

TOUCH AND FEEL THE DIVINITY WITHIN YOU

SRIDEVASENAPATISWAMY

PARTRIDGE
A Penguin Random House Company

To order additional copies of this book, contact
Partridge India
000 800 10062 62
www.partridgepublishing.com/india
orders.india@partridgepublishing.com

Index

Promoter's Remarks

Dear readers,

Namaste.

I am promoter of this book ANTARMUKHI. I am the daughter of the author. I am single child in our small family unit consisting of myself, my mother and my father.

My father is a book lover. The books he goes through are mainly related to philosophy and literature. My father inculcated habit of reading books in me when I was very young. I used to read out and he used to listen, right from the age when I started reading words. During my upper primary and high school days itself I read different books including Shakespeare's plays (which were converted into prose from poetry), many abridged Classics (classics rewritten into small books) apart from some original classics. He encouraged me to read Indian epics in English and Telugu (my mother-tongue). My reading of good books and his listening continued even after completion of my Bachelor's course in engineering. Even when I was doing job, I read out and he listened to the well-known Robin Sharma's book The Monk Who Sold His Ferrari!

I have been observing him practicing yoga from my kindergarten age till this age and learnt some yogasanas from him.

My father's keen interest to study how people look at things is really great. When I was studying my sixth standard, he chose to work as head of a small unit situated in a tribal valley, on behalf of his organization. We left city life and moved to stay there. We were staying in the tribal valley and I was studying in a school there. My father was extensively traveling in the hills and valleys of that area by his scooter, on holidays. After my father worked there as a head of unit of his organization, he has been working since then as head of units of his organization at different far off places.

Sri Prasanna Bharathi Matha Devalayam (Sri Prasanna Bharathi Matha Dhyana Kshetr-a place in the temple earmarked for conducting meditations) is a Temple of Goddess of Knowledge situated in a place where my father was working at the time of writing the original 'Antarmukhi' book of 32 pages. Here my father used to conduct meditation classes every Sunday in evenings. The topics covered in this book are part of those topics touched by my father before and after meditation at that place. Wherever my father conducts meditation, it is habit of my father to perform *'Agnihotram'* (sacred fire) before getting into the actual *Dhyana* (Meditation).

Though I know very well how my father looks at things, it was only after my marriage, I had seen a different angle of my father completely. Even I was surprised as also my mother and our relatives after he wrote a book in Telugu language (this was the original book 'Antarmukhi'). After reading this small book, at the previous work place of my father, a philosopher and scholar called my father over phone, appreciated my father and at the instance of this philosopher and scholar a review meeting was called locally. In this meeting he told that this book of 32 pages is a gist of all philosophical thoughts. He spoke continuously for two hours and he completed review of about one third of this book. He concluded the speech declaring that this small book of 32 pages can be expanded into 320 pages or more. Such is the concept!

My father got great confidence in his spiritual thoughts developed in him over a number of years after his intense practice of meditation for four years during his college days.

Later this book was taken by one of our relatives to Hyderabad. A friend of this relative had taken this book to Dr.C.Narayana Reddy, the well-known Telugu literary luminary, *Gnanapeeth* awardee of Government of India, an Ex-member of Parliament of India and President of *Andhra Saraswat Parishad* (Telugu Literary Academy), Hyderabad. Dr.C.Narayana Reddy, on going through this book, immediately appreciated. This great personality, who is an octogenarian, wrote a letter in his own handwriting appreciating the book and my father's spiritual and literary knowledge. At this same time, my father in law who is a doctorate in Hindi language translated this Telugu book into Hindi. On our request Dr.C.Narayana Reddy released both Telugu and Hindi versions of this book at a function in Hyderabad at the same time. Even after this function, this book was being printed and given by my father freely to his friends, relatives and like-minded people.

After seeing the original book, another relative of our family translated important chapters of this book into English. He also read out the Telugu 'Antarmukhi' Book, voice recorded the same and sent this voice recording to my father through e-mail. This inspired my father to write this book Antarmukhi in English with some additional topics.

My father decided to donate a part of royalties earned by him on this book for the first five years to an international service organization.

The above all inspired me to contact PARTRIDGE INDIA LIMITED. Partridge India Limited is also publishing the Telugu and Hindi versions of the 32 pages book 'Antarmukhi'.

My intention is to make meditation practice and philosophy of my father internationally known.

Introductory Lines to the English Edition

'*ANTARMUKH*' is a Sanskrit word which in
simple terms may be described as:
Turning face inside
Or
Looking into self
(*Antar* = inner, *Mukh* = face)

Because this book tells
about a philosophical method of looking into
self, this book as well as method has been named
'*Antarmukhi*'

In original Telugu book many Sanskrit as well as Telugu words with wide meaning have been mentioned.

The author himself translated the Telugu version into English. In fact in some contexts word to word translation was done from Telugu to English and in some contexts the same Sanskrit or Telugu words were mentioned with the sole intention of keeping the depth of the meaning intact. This attempt may kindly be appreciated.

Dedicated to

The Supreme Commander of this boundless
macro cosmic nucleus
containing
Million billion trillions of cosmic nuclei
The God of gods
The Almighty
and the only One who can bestow right thinking
to
the terrorists, religious fanatics
and
to the
individuals, organizations, systems, and nations
who are suffering from feeling of insecurity and
causing suffering to fellow beings, environment
and to this world.

Thanks

I express my sincere thanks to
Sri Tegalapalli Bala Sanjeeva Reddy
(Retired Industries Promotion Officer,
Industries Department, AP)

16-20, Guddeti Veedhi, Kovelakuntla-518134
(Cell 9000070563)

For
encouraging me and giving suggestions to me in
writing this book

Gratitude

I express my gratitude to the members of:

Sri Prasanna Bharathi Matha Dhyana Kshetr
Sri Prasanna Bharathi Matha Devalayam,
Kovelakuntla
Kurnool District, Andhra Pradesh, INDIA, PIN
518134

Prologue

(READ THIS: DON'T MISS)

Oh! Embodiments of the Supreme Consciousness,

There is a background for bringing this small book to you.

When I was at the age of 15 years, every night I used to sleep on the terrace of my house. Looking at the infinite blue sky, looking at the innumerable stars twinkling on the vast blue screen called sky that too on the nights of moonlight when the beauty of the sky was enriched because of the beautiful moon, enjoying the moonlight, my mind used to undergo an inexplicable thrill and my mind used to experience a kind of joy.

Different kinds of thoughts about this unending universe, and about human life in this world, used to crop up into my mind. Thoughts like "if the God, the creator of this universe appears once to me?" used to come into my mind.

Unknowingly I started getting into a kind of meditation.

After practicing meditation like this for about a year, a kind of flow of spiritual thoughts started in me. My mind used to be full of these spiritual thoughts and experiences and my mind was rather 'choked' with these spiritual thoughts and experiences. I was about 16 years old at that time. There was a very big library near our house.

Curious to know why I was getting these spiritual thoughts, I used to read different books on philosophy.

Surprisingly, I used to find the spiritual thoughts which I had, in those books on philosophy. I used to find even my spiritual experiences mentioned in those books.

Because I had the habit of reading books, I used to read different kinds of books.

But with regard to the spiritual thoughts, I used to find them very peculiar. While all individuals sharpen their spirituality by reading scriptures, through preceptors, and through close association with great personalities, my situation was different from them. My spirituality was sharpened by two. The first one was meditation. The second one was reading scriptures and books on philosophy.

I continued my meditation and I was also going to my college for my regular studies.

At this young age itself I had insight into different kinds of spiritual practices. But no method could impress my mind much.

The peculiar state

But after continuing my meditation for about four years, I found myself in a particular state.

I used to feel that I was near to superhuman powers or supernatural powers.

It used to come to my understanding how the *Saadhaks* mistake some extra sensory powers as super human powers or super natural powers. It also used to come to my understanding why some people call the extra sensory powers as super human powers or super natural powers.

Not only the above. It used to come my understanding how *Saadhaks* will be confused between the extra sensory powers and pure spirituality.

I used to be astonished on my observing how ego of a *Saadhak* would take such a gigantic shape and in front of this gigantic shape of ego, how the size of the Universal Soul of the Lord being worshipped by him would be reduced to the proportions of an atom.

On seeing a *Saadhak* I used to understand the level of his spirituality.

What I say is, the truth about the extra sensory powers is that, for a *Saadhak* who seeks divine path, these extra sensory powers are like witchcraft.

All this is a large screen of mystery beyond one's imagination.

===================================

FOOT NOTE
Saadhaks and Abhyaasaks are those who practice deep meditation techniques like *Kundalini yoga*, *Hatha yoga and Naadi yoga* to reach the state of the eternal bliss.
===================================

The screen of mystery

It used to come to my understanding how a *Saadhak* will be confused to know how much practice will be required to unravel this mystery.

Those who were able to break this large screen of mystery were prophets, thinkers, seekers of truth, visionaries, *yogis* and saints and many other great personalities. That is why humans are worshipping them as representatives of God. They are the representatives of the Universal Consciousness or '*Chetana*' about which I am going to tell you in the coming pages. However, for me, I was not inclined to break this great veil of mystery. I was not inclined to see the other side of this veil. At that time I was 19 years old. Now what I feel is, I had that disinclination because performing of certain other deeds in this life was still left for me.

Fulfillment

Sometimes what I feel is, this life is fulfilled with the spiritual experiences and feelings I had and this is enough for this life. I also used to feel proud because I had understood at least to some extent why the men of knowledge born in this world in different times, at different places and in different beliefs tried to describe that the highest state an individual should attain is the association with God, which is the ultimate and eternal bliss. I also say that pure spirituality is the real glory in an individual's life.

From then on, though I reduced the intensity in practice of meditation, I have been getting spiritual feelings and experiences. I read many books. I heard spiritual discourses of many. More than three decades have also passed since then.

Some years back I felt: If I express my feelings to someone how it looks like and if anyone does spiritual practice like me, how he will be and whether he could get the same great feelings which I had.

There is also a background for my getting this kind of idea in me.

The healer

About seven years back, when I was working in a village on my job, an experience came across me. As I was always busy as a head of a unit, right from morning till night with many financial transactions, and public relations, one day a woman entered my cabin and stood in front of me. She might be around 45 years old. A kind of peace and purity appeared to me in her face. She asked for excuse for having entered my cabin without permission. I asked her what she wanted.

She put an interesting question to me. That was, what was the specialty I had. Initially, I could not understand her question. I looked at her with a question mark. What she again said to me was: "I tried several times to meet you. You were always busy. Today you are alone in the cabin. I came in to talk to you. What is the specialty in you?"

"Why are you asking me this?" I said. As I had a feeling of respect towards her, I told her to sit in a chair in front of my table. She sat in the chair and she said to me with a mark of surprise "you are not like all other persons. There is some difference in you. Do you follow any yoga technique?"

Then I had also come out of my mood of surprise. "Why are you putting this question to me?" I said. She said "answer to my question. Later I will tell you".

I thought for a moment. I told "every morning I practice *yogasanas*. I do meditation. I like reading books. I think everything in the way of spirituality"

Then she said "what I thought is true". A kind of calmness appeared in her face.

Next, she told me about herself. She was an ordinary housewife. She belonged to an agricultural family. She might have studied up to high school level.

The matter was, she was a pranic healer. She knew many healing techniques. She was a middle level pranic healer. She told that she had preceptors who taught these techniques.

The astonishing fact was that her daughters were staying in United States of America and she was able to cure illnesses of her daughters and their kin by sending psychic messages from here.

And she said to me, "certain psychic powers are within you. I have been observing you for the last many days. If you learn these pranic healing techniques, you can cure many of their illnesses. You can make many people get rid of their health problems".

She told that she would give me addresses and phone numbers of her preceptors.

I told her that, in view of my job, it would be difficult for me to allocate time for such skills. I told her that I would not be able to do justice even if I learnt such techniques.

Since then, she met me at my workplace twice or thrice. Once, when she met me she gave me phone numbers and addresses of her preceptors.

When she came another time, what she told me was that I should learn these pranic healing techniques at least to cure myself of my illnesses.

After some days, I left that place on transfer and went to another place. However there was a reason for my not showing interest in such healing techniques. In fact, I had faced many critical situations in matters of ill health in my life. I overcame them. I was able to overcome not because of my power of meditation. I overcame simply through nature cure techniques, fasting and through fine homoeopathic treatments.

Power of meditation is fantastic. Once or twice I put myself to test. Power of meditation is a fantastic power. The power of the divine or the *Chetana* that is spread across the universe is the power of equilibrium in this universe. If we invoke that power of equilibrium, is there anything that cannot be achieved?

What I think is some *Saadhaks, Abhyaasaks* or those who exhibit extra physical powers or extra psychic powers, with the practice of the art

14

of stimulating and invoking some power in this universe, either divert the course of flow of that power, or centralize that power at a place.

However, what I think is, the prophets, great saints and yogis, and great devotees of God might have got such powers unknowingly without their desire to acquire them or accidentally. The divine power within them might have been transformed into a stimulating power or a driving force for happenings of some wonders. All such happenings seem happenings because of divine powers or miracles to ordinary people. However, because the aim of these great personalities is the association with God, the Almighty, they might have paid least attention to exhibition of such powers.

What I also think is, spirituality in an individual's life is an incomparable glory in his life and any fortune is next to this.

And also, what I think is individual gets liberation not through acquiring divine powers. It is possible only through making his individual force to dissolve in the force that is spread across the universe.

Conclusion to prolouge

Before I started practicing meditation, and till I reached the age of 14-15 years, in view of my domestic circumstances, I used to be very discouraged in all respects. I failed in my school final exam. I passed school final, because of moderation marks added by government. But I passed my degree exams in first division. I was college topper. This was all because of the greatness of meditation.

I think that meditation should become part of life of everyone.

I feel that, right from the stage of studentship, in all ages, every individual should make meditation a part in his life. My meditation practice never discouraged me in any difficult situation. My meditation does not advise me to be away from my duties. In fact meditation internally advises any one to accomplish duties early in life and also enthusiastically.

My spirituality completely contradicts running away from duties.

Through mediation, an individual develops in him a balanced view and a balanced approach.

Hence my wish is that, this meditation should be made familiar to every individual as a movement. My aspiration is to convert this practice of meditation into a movement.

My dream is that the shape of this world will change by bringing in pure spirituality and progressive thinking, because pure spirituality of an individual is foundation not only to enlightenment of himself but also to enlightenment of the society.

Hence I am bringing this small book to you.

With regards,

Sridevasenapatiswamy

Sri Prasanna Bharathi Matha Dhyana Kshetr
(Sri Prasanna Bharathi Matha Devalayam)
Kovelakuntla
Kurnool District, Andhra Pradesh.
PIN 518134
India

Meditation

For meditation concentration is required.
For concentration contentment and feeling of
fulfillment is required.

How can, a mind which is
not contented and a mind which desires more and
more, attain a state of concentration?

For this state of discontentment and
unfulfilled state the main reason is the desires
that are not satisfied and feeling of insecurity.

For satisfying the desires duties and deeds
are to be performed and performing these, mind
thinks in different ways.

These are the distractions against reaching the state of concentration.

Concentration is possible only if necessities and duties are regulated.

The security ring

Is it not that we enter a security ring when we take our mind to the proximity of God in meditation?

If we are still with the feeling of insecurity, what it means is that, we do not have belief that God is answer to everything.

That means we have not entered the security ring called the Proximity of God.

Is it not that true meditation should take us into the security ring called Proximity of God?

It is the real mediation that takes us into the security ring and keeps us peaceful.

Why is meditation required?

According to Hindu spiritual thoughts, in this creation, every creature is experiencing the results of its own deeds and every creature as per the deeds of its earlier birth is taking the present birth. The soul in the creature is revolving in the cycle of births and deaths. He is becoming the cause of good deeds or bad deeds. This soul should, at some point of time, get out of this cycle of pleasures, pains, happiness, sorrow, suffering, fears, again good deeds and again bad deeds. Such strong desire to get out of this cycle will take shape in every creature at some point of time and at some stage in this cycle of births and deaths.

In every birth, instead of taking some life form, experiencing the pleasures and pains, fears, suffering, and instead of experiencing the results of good deeds and bad deeds, a desire to reach a state emanates, a state of existing in all living and nonliving, being one with the '*Chetana*' which is spread across this universe, which cannot be bound by results of good deeds and bad deeds and to reach a state which cannot be described in qualities, characteristics or in any manner.

Such a desire is aspiration for liberation and such *Chetana* which is spread across this universe is the Supreme soul or the Universal Consciousness.

To reach this state, we should establish a link between us and God. Such link is established through practice of meditation. After sometime, when nature takes back our physical body from us, with this link established through practice of meditation, let us deliver our soul to the Supreme Soul. Let us become one with the Supreme Soul. This is the desire for liberation.

Such a state which we will achieve is the Supreme state of Oneness.

Hence meditation is required.

This is for whom?

Feeling of an individual to reach such state of liberation or a state of Oneness is beyond the boundaries of religion, caste and creed. This is beyond one's possessions, wealth, high positions in society and any other status. It is not related to level of education of an individual, because all these are related to this birth or this life.

Scholarly knowledge is related to this birth or life.

Spiritual knowledge is related to a state that is beyond births.

Spiritual knowledge is that one which takes us to the state of Oneness or liberation.

A state which is called by Hindus as liberation or the state of Oneness is called Kingdom of God by some other religion. Some other religions are calling this state with some other name.

Such men of divine knowledge who are aspiring the above state are in all religions. Such men of divine knowledge are in the rich. They are in the poor. They are in literates and illiterates. Men of such divine knowledge are in the people whom we term then as civilized. Such men of divine knowledge are in uncivilized people also. They are in palaces and forests. Such men of divine knowledge are everywhere in this world. Hence meditation is meant for those who are aspiring the divine knowledge and thereby the state of liberation or the state of Oneness. Meditation is meant for such individuals only.

What happens if an individual turns 'Antarmukh'?

Mind gets stability.
Mind attains the state of peace.
Mind does not think sideways

Because an individual knows the aim of his life, quality in his discretion and perception will improve. For getting out of the cycle of good deeds, bad deeds, pleasures, pains, fears, sufferings first the individual identifies his duties. He will try to discharge his duties with great skill corresponding to his age, i.e., adolescence, youth and old age, because if one does not perform one's duties well, will it not mean, a bad deed? Will it not lead to other bad deeds?

In fact not performing duties properly is a bad deed. A student's aim will be only acquiring knowledge. Man or woman after having formed a family of his or her own, will discharge his or her domestic responsibilities well, because if duties or responsibilities are not discharged properly, would not they remain as bondages or rather bad deeds? Would not one again have to necessarily complete these unfinished deeds?

In society also, the individuals whose aim is association of God, will discharge their duties and responsibilities in such a fashion and with such a skill and intelligence that they should not again wriggle or struggle to get out of these bondages.

These persons enjoy all the comforts that come to them during the course of discharging their duties. With the same mind they accept all the discomforts and sorrows. These persons stand like a rock in times of adversity. They are not moved by any criticisms. They will not be afraid of difficulties. They will not be inflated by flattery. They do not feel happy on getting recognitions, because the recognitions they want are not related to this world. The recognition they expect is from the Supreme Soul to be eligible to join Him.

When the persons are getting such recognitions from the Supreme Soul and they are reaching the state which is beyond time, cycle of births and deaths, and characteristics, why should they run for some recognitions which are related to and bound by the time, and recognitions connected to this birth?

Similarly, when an individual himself is going to become the Supreme Soul who is containing all the identities within Himself, why should the individual run for the worldly identities?

The individual who becomes '*Antarmukh*' will be astonished and feels happy on seeing his reflection within himself and the belief, that his personality made and identified by his family and society is true, will vanish.

He will establish the truth in himself that his personality is divine which is beyond time, births and characteristics.

What is the meaning of 'identifying one's self with the divine that is beyond time, births and characteristics'?

Time is formed on rotation of the planet earth around itself and revolving around the Sun in this solar system. To tell broadly, the yardstick for time is simply the number of times the planet earth is rotating itself and revolving around the Sun. Is it not that the seasons are occurring only because of the rotation of the earth and revolving around the sun?

If we travel and go out of the solar system, there is neither day nor night. There are no seasons. There is no time at all. Hence that which is outside this solar system is not bound by time. But even outside this solar system there is an existence or a power. Is it not?

This power is above all the planets in this solar system and above all other solar systems, if there are any such systems in this universe. All these planets, solar systems and stars are subject to this power. And I say that this power is within us also, because these solar systems are subjected to this power and we are living on a planet which is bound by time scheduled in this solar system. Is it not? Hence I feel that we are not simply this physical body being maintained by the crops grown through happening of seasons bound by time. I say that there is an unidentified power or existence or 'Chetana' which is spread across the universe and this is within us also.

To describe 'which is beyond birth', according to the Hindu philosophical thinking every creature is taking its birth basing on the deeds performed in its earlier life. Basing on the deeds performed in this life, it is getting next life. However, whatever may be the births or no matter how many forms that a creature may have, there is one factor constant in all these births. Whatever may be the behavior of this creature basing on the existing values when it has taken birth and basing on the place where it has taken birth, there is one constant factor flowing through all these births. That factor is the soul which was separated from the Supreme Soul. And whatever we learn in this birth is related to this birth only. Scientific knowledge acquired in this birth will vanish at the end of this life. At last, the soul which is separated from the 'Chetana' will remain.

'Beyond characteristics' means different kinds of thoughts, and the characteristics which are basis for these thoughts, might have emanated from the basic instincts of the earlier births, many thoughts emanate because of the environment in which we are moving around. However the 'Chetana' which is spread across this universe has contained all these different kinds of characteristics within itself, because this Chetana reflects in all the creatures and after these characteristics disappear, it is only the Chetana that remains.

Another important point is that everyone's individuality and his way of thinking mainly depend on the conditions of his family and the social conditions and the social values existing in the time when that individual has taken birth, and the values which are the deciding factors for the personality development contemplated in that particular time.

However whatever may be the values existing in any point of time, there is a permanent truth beyond all these values. Such truth is never bound by the values of a particular time and is never bound by the social conditions existing in a particular time. Such and certain truth which is above all these values and conditions is *'Chetana'*.

Every individual aspires to have an identity for himself in the society where he lives. He aspires to reach the highest stage in the values which are recognized by his family and the society. He feels that his life is fulfilled on reaching the stage which he assumed basing on the values created in him by his family and society. But this individual will be astonished at his own running race when he recognizes the *'Chetana'* which contains all the identities within itself.

Similarly, every individual will form a compass of his own basing on the values formed in him and he looks at this world through the directions of this compass. Every individual has his own compass. But when the values themselves are not permanent, can we say that the compass formed for him by himself be contemplated as a right measure to verify the ultimate truth?

Similarly, deciding the divinity with the yardstick formed with the present values, and trying to measure the *'Chetana'* which is spread across this universe, and which is beyond time is not proper. Is it?

And there are different theories about the birth of this mankind and birth of life force on the earth which occurred prior to onset of civilizations and their progress. Different religions are also proposing their own theories. However these different civilizations corresponding to their respective geographical conditions and other factors have formed their own gods.

For all religious beliefs, earth is the center point for all their thoughts and imaginations. In their view, gods formed by their civilizations and religions are rulers of this universe. But, there was an existence in this universe even before the gods were formed by these civilizations and religions. Is it not true? The gods and goddesses of the present time may not exist after passage of time. On change in the way of thinking in the civilizations, in course of time, new gods may take birth and new theories may be formed. Worshipping is also being done to these gods according to the geological conditions of that particular place where such gods are worshipped. Is it not?

For example, I think, in the Indian subcontinent which is the center for Hindu religion, gods of forces of nature were worshipped more. At one time performing of rituals such as *Yagna, Yaga and Havan* was in prominence, because the economy in the Indian subcontinent was mainly dependent on rains and winds of monsoon and mainly these rituals were performed for rains and to praise gods and superior gods, who according to the beliefs in this religion, are controlling the forces of nature.

Lastly to describe the '*Chetana*', as a matter of fantasy, it can be said that this '*Chetana*' is an enormous shape of power which can swallow the time, civilizations, gods, different qualities of gods, characteristics and values at once.

When we attempt to personify this *Chetana*, the thought or image that we form in our mind is GOD.

We may also infer that the Brahma matter which is referred in Hindu scriptures as that which is beyond one's specific imagination or description is '*Chetana*'.

An individual, on becoming *Antarmukh*, should identify himself as that '*Chetana*'

Chetana—Brahma matter—Supreme Soul—the Supreme Logic

I want to tell something about *Chetana*, Brahma Matter, and the Supreme Soul. In general sense all these three represent the Supreme Consciousness or Universal Consciousness.

In ancient India, a sage propagated a number of principles about this Brahma matter. The principles propagated by the sage are about 555!

Even without referring to those principles, I believe that all the above terms represent the large web that is spread across the universe, to say in simple terms. To imagine further we can say that this large web was woven by the Master Weaver God himself.

No one knows the beginning or the corners of this unending web.

It is also difficult to conclude whether God is separate from this web or he is himself part of it adjusting this universe to one Supreme logic and taking care of everything. In fact there is an argument that this universe what we see or feel in the form of nature is a manifestation of God himself and He, hence has two faces and the other face is completely beyond one's specific imagination, and if at all we wish to reach him, it will be possible through this nature only and through this physical body only.

It is also difficult to conclude whether the nature which is seen by us is only a physical force or if there is a separate force that stimulates this physical force.

No one knows whereabouts of this unending motor because nothing is permanent in this universe and this universe manifests itself continuously.

The Brahma matter is in no way connected to the time being observed by the life force on this planet earth because time is subjected to this earth and this solar system only and we do not know if there is any Super Time. This Brahma matter is in no way connected to the human mind, animal mind or feelings of any life force.

The forces of nature on this planet earth are limited to this planet only. Gods, worshipping of different gods, different religious beliefs make parts of the civilizations that took place on this planet earth only. The social values, customs, traditions being followed are parts of the civilizations that happened on this planet only. As already told, the values are ever changing.

We are able to know through recorded findings about the human life and its culture and about happenings on this earth, probably about the happenings dated back to 10000 BC utmost. If we imagine about the future happenings on this earth and the civilizations that will take place in the coming millions of years, we do not know where we end in thinking.

It looks silly when we think back about the kings, wars waged by them, slavery, struggles of humans for freedoms in different forms, and the strife faced by the humans all these centuries.

The human race on this planet is struggling for its own dignified living. Can we imagine whether this human race will ever think of understanding Supreme logic of this universe in which everything including the nonliving, on this planet exits with dignity?

Now we are seeing or rather feeling this universe with our physical body which lives for about 100 years at the most. We are trying to maintain our physical bodies here for the present, we are trying to adhere to the values and beliefs of today and we are also trying to live up to the recognized social, cultural and economic values of today. All these are limited to this planet earth only.

I feel that there is a separate astral body for every individual, which is in no way connected to the life, life values of this planet earth. I also feel that good deeds or bad deeds that a soul or the astral body is involved in are not related to the values of a particular time but they are related to a certain Supreme logic.

The astral body is part of the large web woven by the Master Weaver God.

The actual LIBERATION from all struggles happens only when we feel that we are part of that large web, whatever we try to establish on this planet is only temporary and for this we are causing others to suffer. By bringing this understanding this entire human race will be first liberated from struggle and strife, and every individual will have LIBERATION, in fact in philosophical sense also.

Now if human race can live up to dignity, then this human race can think of leaving everything on this earth to live in dignity, understanding the Supreme logic.

The actual LIBERATION takes place when the entire human race understands true God and then his logic.

I feel that in every religion this concept of the Supreme logic exists and this should be brought to the fore. In fact the prophets, saints and other great personalities tried their best to make the humanity understand this Supreme logic and in pursuit of this they were persecuted and even killed. We all know that if any harm was done to them or any trouble was caused to them, it was done to their physical bodies only.

I feel that, for understanding their Supreme logic, meditation is the only KEY.

Manifested—Unmanifested— the Universal Consciousness

We always think that what is seen is what exists and nothing more than that. Do we ever think that what is not seen is more than what is seen?

In a well-known Hindu scripture a concept about this manifestation was put forward very simply like this:

"BEINGS ARE UNMANIFEST IN THE BEGINNING, MANIFEST IN THE MIDDLE AND BECOME UNMANIFEST IN THE END"

I also say that this world is a continuous manifestation of itself and nobody knows when this manifestation began and when it ends. As already told no one knows whereabouts of this unending motor.

It is also said that there is a Universal Consciousness which is source for these states of manifest, and unmanifest. As also already told this Universal Consciousness is the Brahma matter and this is not related to human mind. This Universal Consciousness is above all whether living or nonliving, existing or non-existing, seen or not seen, felt or not felt.

I also say that one should identify oneself with this Universal Consciousness which is the source for both manifest and unmanifest.

The above state is the Liberation or the Supreme state of Oneness.

This may otherwise be said as a permanent unmanifested state of Universal Consciousness, the state in which the soul will not take birth again, and again get into the unending cycle of births and deaths.

I say that this concept of Universal Consciousness is really fascinating.

Manifestation of individual soul—man's search for identity

As has been said earlier that this universe is the manifestation of the Supreme soul, the individual physical body and its actions are also manifestations of the individual soul.

It can be further said that in fact every human being is in search of its identity. While every human-being after its primary desires are satisfied, is searching for its own identity. The individual is running for recognitions. His desire for higher recognitions or higher identities never stops. In fact every human being will be happy once it gets the recognition which it aspires but this human being wants further higher identities.

There is no end for this. Different human beings want different kinds of recognitions.

The individual's quest for further and further recognitions stops when he realizes that there is only one identity, he should recognize himself with the Supreme Soul which is containing all the identities within itself.

In a well-known scripture, the 'incarnation of the Lord' says that all the superior forms in this universe are his manifestations only and once a soul reaches him, the soul's desire to acquire greater forms or identities stops. Hence 'the incarnation of the Lord' says, if a soul attains Him, it is equal to attaining all possessions, or superior forms at once. Here the different manifestations of the individual come to an end.

The real, the unreal, illusion, true knowledge

The concept that this world is unreal is very interesting. According to this concept this world what we see or feel is not permanent and it is ever changing. The only real one is the *Chetana* or the Supreme Consciousness which is manifesting itself as the world which we are seeing or feeling.

The individual soul is in fact is in search of its identity, only to rejoin its origin but due to the distractions, individual soul after it acquires a separate physical body is under an 'illusion'. The mind for which base is the physical body deceives and misleads the individual and the individual becomes cause to good deeds and bad deeds and revolves in the cycle of births and deaths. The only solution to rejoin the Supreme Soul is to understand this reality and understanding this reality is called the 'true knowledge'. For reaching this state of 'true knowledge' the individual should exercise his 'discrimination' to identify the real and unreal and to reach the 'real'.

I am also bringing forward this concept because this concept helps one to understand the '*Chetana*' or the Supreme Consciousness.

The individual, to reach the above state, before understanding the nature of the Supreme Consciousness should know what he really is.

TO UNDERSTAND THIS, AN INDIVIDUAL SHOULD GO DEEP INTO HIMSELF AND HE SHOULD COME TO AN UNDERSTANDING THAT HIS INDIVIDUAL SOUL IS NOTHING BUT PART OF THE SUPREME SOUL.

Some men of knowledge say that coming to this understanding itself is the state of Liberation or the Supreme state of Oneness.

There exists a Supreme power from which every individual power is drawing its power—what to meditate upon ultimately?

In one of the ancient Indian scriptures, a concept was told, according to which there is only one common power ultimately from which all individual powers draw their powers. The illustrative description goes like this. Once gods won in a battle fought with demons and they were celebrating victory. Suddenly a spirit appeared to them and the gods could not guess who that spirit was. The spirit threw a dry blade of grass in front of the gods of nature—the god of air, the god of fire, and the god of water, challenged them to blow it, burn it, and soak it respectively. These three gods could not do anything at their will though they tried their best to blow it, burn it, and soak it respectively.

Then the mother of the universe who represents the physical form of this nature tells them that there is 'father' who gives energy to everyone and he is the ultimate force.

In meditation we concentrate on this ultimate force.

Soul and its transformation or 'wearing different bodies one after one'

This entire universe is a single unit. In this unit continuous manifestation is going on.

In this unit the feeling of 'I' is not going anywhere but is wearing different bodies one after one basing on the deeds it performed in its earlier lives. This transformation is a continuous process.

In ancient India, many interpretations were made as to what kind of life a soul takes or the body it wears in next life. When I was young I used to see even the charts prepared by some believers depicting what kind of person will wear which kind of body or life form in his next life!

However in a famous Indian scripture, the 'God's Incarnation' says that the soul takes its form in next life depending on the thought the individual is involved in, at the time of leaving the present body. (Here it is impossible to interpret what an individual is thinking at the time of leaving the present body and even if at all if we can interpret, it is impossible to guess the next life form of that individual). Hence the 'God's incarnation' says that, to reach Him, an individual's mind, at the time of leaving the present body should be filled with the thought about Him only to attain Him, whose abode is the supreme abode.

Is meditation a stop-thought process or a trance?

I say that the meditation is none of the above.

While the aim of meditation is to know about the self, supreme self and to reach the Supreme state of Oneness ultimately, it is neither a stop-thought process nor a trance.

Meditation starts with an inquest to know the real 'I' and the 'Supreme I'. There is no method to get down to meditation straight away.

In fact thoughts start to pour in. Slowly, the thoughts settle and calmness starts prevailing upon the mind. Next it goes to further stillness. It is the stillness of the mind, where the feeling of 'I' starts, because it is basic feeling 'I' which is between the 'Supreme I' and the individual's thought process. When you go to the base of the feeling 'I', your 'I' points at the 'Supreme I' and there will be nothing but the "Supreme I" which is across this universe. Once your 'I' touches the Supreme 'I', the individual 'I' unfolds and spreads across this universe and this is the state which is called the Supreme state of Oneness.

I advise every individual who tries to practice this to be careful and cautious in getting into meditation. It should be a very slow process and no one should try to do any 'practicals' with this, because it is the human mind ultimately which has to absorb the waves that emanate in meditation. Do not imagine of becoming something.

Stopping of thoughts forcefully will not be of much use and this kind of mental exercise may cause some trouble to the mind.

We often hear some scholars say that the mental state of an individual who reached the Supreme state of the divine will be like that of trance. In fact no state of trance is meditation and through meditation one will not enter into any trance. If at all if anyone is in such kind of trance, it is only a trance or rather an illusion. Hence a state of trance should never be called meditation or result of meditation.

The concept of Supreme Consciousness is not against any religious belief or any god of any religion.

The concept of '*Chetana*' or the Supreme Consciousness is not against any religious belief or any god of any religion, because the ultimate goal of any religious belief or religious practitioner is to reach the abode of the Supreme Lord only.

My effort through this book is to stress that the goal of every religious practice or practitioner can be realized through meditation quickly and they can enjoy the sweetness of the great religious thoughts which their respective great personalities professed.

My effort through this book is not against any gods of any religion because I believe that every god is a facet of the Supreme Lord. The unknown intellectual who found a particular God must have tasted sweetness in worshipping of that particular facet of the Supreme Lord.

We should bow to each and every god of every religion because every god is nothing but a facet of the Supreme Lord.

Mind, intellect and the soul

Along with the physical body, an individual also consists of mind, intellect and the soul.

The above three are in the ascending order.

While the base of mind is the physical body and simply acts as per the directions of the physical body, the intellect uses the discretion. It is the soul that enjoys or suffers from the results of the discretion.

It can also be said that mind and intellect are the two pillars which are holding the soul high. The intellect is at the higher level and because of its discretion the soul will be either rejuvenated or degenerated. While mind tries to upkeep the body the intellect tries to upkeep the soul.

I wish to illustrate the above logic which is applicable not only to an individual but also family, institution, society, community, system, organization or even to a nation.

Mind is like a corporeal head and intellect is a spiritual head of any unit right from a family to a nation. Soul of an individual will degenerate when the mind and intellect of any individual do not get along.

Soul of any family, institution, society, community, system, organization or even the nation is its heritage only. Just like an individual's mind and intellect getting along to keep the soul healthy, I feel that both the corporeal and spiritual heads should get along to keep the soul of any unit of the above, right from the family to the nation healthy. While the corporeal head tries to regulate the physical lives of its people, the spiritual head tries to regulate the social and spiritual lives of its people. Hence I feel in respect of every unit up to the national level, in some form or other, the concept of 'the Crown and the Church' exists.

Just like in some occasions when the mind overtakes the intellect and impulsive acts start dominating the life of the individual leading to ultimate degeneration of the soul, or when the intellect overtakes the mind the importance of the physical existence is subdued, it also happens in case of units right from family to the nation.

Mind, intellect and the soul (continued)

If we go back into the pages of history, we can observe that the institutions right from a family to a nation destroyed themselves due to absence of intellectual discretion. The 'Church' part of the unit was subdued or destroyed and ultimately that led to the destruction of the unit itself.

Even in recent pages of history the 'Church' part of those nations were destroyed by their corporeal heads, and ultimately many families were shattered, societies were shattered, traditions were destroyed, organizations were destroyed, age old institutions were destroyed, cultural groups were shattered, spiritual groups were shattered and the ruthless efforts of these corporeal heads to give a facelift to their nation, by forming artificial groups of these in place of the age old original, which was correct in their view, resulted in defacing of the entire social, cultural and spiritual structures of those nations. Ultimately souls of these nations were degenerated because their soul is their cultural and spiritual heritage only. These nations had to face many upheavals—cultural, social, economic, political and even in respect of geographical identity.

Even in respect of an individual, both mind and intellect should play their roles to keep the soul healthy. Only a healthy soul can reach the Supreme Soul.

Spirituality in an individual's life is an incomparable glory and any fortune is next to this

        Here 'spirituality in an individual's life' means 'true knowledge to reach the Supreme Soul'

I say that this is a glory in an individual's life because it is the true knowledge that takes any person to the proximity of the Supreme Soul.

In one of the scriptures in Hindu religion, in his concluding verses, the author says that the state of the person who is blessed with true knowledge to reach the Supreme Soul can be compared to that of an emperor who is in full youth, beautiful, educated, healthy, with a strong will power, with great army to conquer anything, blessed with all kinds of wealth and enjoying all pleasures which a human aspires to enjoy. Yet, the author further says that the emperor who enjoys all these cannot be equally compared to the person who is blessed with the true knowledge because the emperor might have acquired all kinds of wealth etc. by performing certain deeds and he may have to undergo results later in next life, but the person who is blessed with true knowledge reaches the Supreme Soul or is already enjoying the state of being with the Supreme Soul without having to undergo any results in next life, because there will not be next life once he reaches the abode of the Supreme Lord.

An individual's aspiration to become a leader or to lead a group

To say philosophically, if one has any desire to be a leader or to lead a group it means that there are certain deeds yet to be performed in this life and for this again he has to undergo results in next life. If at all this individual becomes a leader, he may be leader of a small group in this large universe for a minutest part of time in this unending time. In course of performing the duties of a leader he has to perform certain deeds knowingly or unknowingly and he has to undergo results again in his next life.

Irrespective of one's desire to become a leader, if one wishes to reach the Supreme Soul, one's goal will be the highest and one will become the leader of this universe!

Can an individual's successes in this worldly life be linked to his spirituality?

What is this unknown factor which decides the final result?

Spirituality in this context means 'true spiritual knowledge to reach the Supreme soul'. I say that an individual's successes in this worldly life need not be linked to one's spirituality. In fact, because a spiritual person's goal is different he will not be disturbed by any failures in this material world.

One's success in this material life depends on many factors and for success one has to put in many efforts physically and mentally, in the material world.

The baffling aspect is the unknown factor, which every individual is afraid of. This unknown factor is otherwise the uncertainty about the final result. This unknown factor is referred as God.

However a spiritual person's discretion or logic will be completely different and common people who are in pursuit of successes in this material world may not be able to understand the logic of the spiritual persons, but as we are seeing, ultimately the spiritual person's logic is proved to be the truth. That is why logic of the great personalities prevailed ultimately and permanently though they failed temporarily in the material world.

In a well-known Hindu scripture, the 'God's incarnation' says that even if a spiritual person cannot reach him during his life time because of many distractions, he will take birth again in a comfortable family to continue his spiritual pursuit to reach the Supreme Abode.

ABOVE ALL, STRENGTH OF A SPIRITUAL
PERSON IS HIS RIGHTIOUSNESS AND THIS
IS THE UNKNOWN STRENGTH GIVEN TO
HIM BY GOD HIMSELF.

My Spiritual practice

    I mentioned about the screen of mystery in the beginning pages of this book (in prologue). I want to tell something more about this screen of mystery.

During the period when I was in the age of about 15 to 19 years, I reached a peak level in my spiritual practice. In these years I was in my college studies. I mentioned that I used to do meditation in the nights on the terrace of my house. Apart from this, during the days of rain and severe winter, when it was not possible for me to do meditation on the terrace of my house, I used to go to my college playground which was very near to my house and I used to do meditation there. Playground of our college was very large and adjoining this, there was a large area of greenery and many trees including many tamarind trees. The college buildings and large college ground and the large of area of greenery and trees were once part of the palaces of the kings of Hyderabad. I used to sit somewhere and meditate, and sometimes even stand somewhere and meditate. I used to enjoy the calmness walking through those large areas alone in the evenings. Even in day times, during holidays I used go to the college ground, sit under a tree and spend my time reading some books, either my text books or some other books of interest. I was staying with my eldest brother who was my care taker. In our house, I, my eldest brother, my sister in law and my younger sister were staying. I was never involved by them in any of our domestic chores. I was left free and my eldest brother was having great belief in me with regard to my behavior. Hence the entire time of the day was at my disposal. When there was some urgent domestic work in which my presence was required, my brother used to ask me, if I could spare some time for him specially!

After my college study hours, I used to spend most of my time in the large library which was near to our house, because in this library there was text book section also and I was also having the opportunity of going through books written by different authors on each subject and in fact during my entire college studies, I did not purchase any text books.

I sometimes think that this kind of life helped me a lot to devote time and develop a kind of spiritual practice because I was also without any responsibilities and any kind of tensions personally. My aim was on two matters. One was my studies and the other was spirituality and my spiritual practice. I feel that this kind of life was a gift to me from God.

At the age of 16 years I studied the Bhagavad-Gita and the New Testament. I also read books on Lord Buddha and I had also gone through quotations of the other prophets and great religions leaders and thinkers. Lord Buddha, only after having made a long journey 'within himself', started preaching. The great prophet Mohammed was living with the Divine, though he was living a simple and common man's life and he had to undergo many sufferings like any commoner. I was also influenced by the great prophets who taught the people to live with the divine and also to live with dignity and valor. In fact there are a number of shining stars as well as twinkling stars in the sky of spirituality.

I was greatly influenced by great personalities Lord Krishna and Lord Jesus Christ. I used to go through religious magazines and different books on spirituality and also many Indian scriptures. As the library where I used to read books, was a very big library I used to go through and also used to refer local, national and international magazines and periodicals on different subjects. As politics and economics were subjects in my college studies, I used to read a number of books on politics, political systems, economic systems and world history, and also biographies of great personalities and thinkers. I was also reading many literary works. Because of this, in my college I used to bag prizes regularly in literary competitions and I became popular in my college.

However my friends' group always used to look at me with curiosity and with a difference because the way I used to look at issues, the way I used to analyze and the way I used to conclude was entirely different. The funny or humorous side of the issues I used to look at and analyze was being received well but sometimes this was also annoying my friends or colleagues.

During my college days, a radical group tried to woo me into their fold. They were regularly visiting my college, they used to wish me and start some kind of conversation on different social issues and they started visiting my house also on some pretext. They had taken me twice to our college ground and they explained to me about their ideologies. Third time when I started to tell them that their views were not correct and there was a kind of an argument between me and them. Later they declared that I was not right person to join their movement and they were never seen again during my college days.

At the same time because of regular practice of a kind of meditation, apart from being young I was at the peak of my physical and mental abilities. Apart my being in the age of adolescence, even my voice used to be like a metallic voice and my friends used to advise me to learn music vocal. I used to have great remembrance power. I used to feel that I was having a kind of clairvoyance. I was having a feeling that one can fly in the air through regular spiritual practice, one can walk on water, one can do miracles because doing a miracle is nothing but a simple act of transfer of your individual energy into the common universal energy and this common universal energy can stimulate any matter or any non-matter at your will because the extended energy of yours and the energy that is stimulated becomes ultimately your energy only, and because ultimately there is only one energy which is being blown into different forms (This interpretation is not of now made by me but I used to think this when I was actually at the height of my spiritual practice). I used to feel that learning any art, including literature and music was not difficult. I used to feel that the mind was opened up and was showing up all kinds of inherent energies. I used to feel that, with this kind of mental and physical energies only, the great personalities who influenced the mankind were moving around on this earth.

Scientific temper and screen of mystery

At that time, I had rather a jolt in my way of spiritual thinking. One day there was a news item in all national newspapers. The then Prime Minister of our country gave a general exhortation that every citizen should develop 'scientific temper'. This sent chills into me. I questioned myself whether all my feelings were scientifically correct or not. In fact, for this question there was no answer. I was continuing my meditation, but I started reading some books of psychology. I was questioning myself whether the spiritual feelings or divine feelings were simply matter based, but I was getting a kind of spiritual satisfaction which the noble men used to call the 'true and ultimate knowledge'. At the same time I was also reasoning to myself that sweetness in eating sugar is different from sweetness of the feeling of being in association of God. Were all great feelings of all those noble men simple imaginations? Should all those spiritual feelings and the so called self-realizations and visualizations be considered as simple illusions or otherwise in terms of atheists 'hallucinations'?

Apart my reading books on different religious practices, I visited some spiritual centers who were advocating their own way of interpretation about God and their own way of spiritual practice.

I also attended discourses of some spiritual leaders. Finally I decided to continue my own way of understanding in furthering my spiritual practice.

I completed three fourths of my college studies, and I was also worried as to how I would make my livelihood in view of the unemployment conditions prevailing then. As I belonged to a large family, I was having intense desire to settle in some job or profession immediately after completion of my college studies. With this intention only, I acquired two technical qualifications simultaneously when I was in my college studies itself and I became psychologically comfortable with a feeling that I would not be left unemployed after I left my college (Later, I got employment immediately after I completed my college studies, with the help of these two skills). At the time when I acquired the technical skills, I was also at the height of practice of my meditation. I was good at my regular studies, and in fact I was one of the bright students in my class, but sometimes my close friends used to question me why I was not like other students and other teenagers and why I was looking at things in a different angle. I was not able to answer. However slowly I started to question myself whether my way of looking at things would suit in the material world, because as a student I was living in my own world and my world was a special world of spiritual understanding which cannot be explained in words.

As you Know, ONLY A FEW PEOPLE SAW IT, AND THOSE WHO SAW IT COULD NOT EXPLAIN IT!

After about three months of deep conflict in my mind, I decided to think like any normal person, like a teenager. I also decided to think and to look at things like any ordinary individual who thinks, looks at things and also behaves in tune with the surroundings, circumstances, necessities, morals and standards etc. I decided to be a common man though I had been blessed with uncommon feelings.

Then I understood why it is said that only a few people saw it and those who saw it could not explain it! It is a large screen of mystery between matter and non-matter. It is the screen between the seen and the unseen. I feel that the great personalities walked freely on both sides of the screen because they found no difference between their existence and nonexistence because they had seen what is going to permanently exist and they identified themselves with that permanence and their very material existence was not a matter to them.

While ordinary people saw manifestation of matter, those noble men saw the manifestation of non-matter just like they saw any material. They found no difference between living and non-living. Hence there is no death for them. The nourishment which these noble personalities get is not from the temporary materials for their temporary bodies. I think this is immortality.

I felt that with further spiritual practice, I could have reached that stage but I did not dare it. Self-realization is the only way to understand the link between the matter and non-matter because there is no material instrument to measure the non-matter and as on today there is no specific 'scientific approach' for that. Hence it is still a mystery. When manifestation of the matter itself is still a mystery to mankind, when can mankind solve the mystery of the non-matter? I feel that any spiritual practitioner would be like me in dilemma because he does not know as to how much practice would be required to cross this screen. Only the prophets and other great personalities either correctly guessed it or daringly crossed it.

MY RETREAT STARTED.

Retreat, slide, stride

When I looked back, I understood that unknowingly I was climbing a very high mountain and that in fact I crossed many peaks and this is the mountain from top of which you could touch the sky. So I was looking at this world from such a top and the feelings I had all these days were real because I have to reach the ground again. Again I was in dilemma, I thought once again, what if I continue climbing this great mountain and touch the sky which was the goal of any being and about which the scriptures of all religions said that this should be aspiration of every individual. Again, I did not dare to continue. I decided to climb down.

I thought that climbing down would be like a slide. But I reached the ground in strides. I was on the ground! This experience cannot be forgotten. I decided to preserve this experience within my soul. I showcased it for myself!

Since then I have been doing meditation and linking myself to the Supreme Consciousness but not with so much intensity and with such deep meditation, as I was doing in those four years.

Desire to wear kumkum on my forehead during the 4 years of my intense practice of meditation

Here I wish to tell one interesting feature I observed during the four years of my intense practice of meditation.

I was having desire to wear kumkum (red) on my fore head just above middle of my eye brows. During the four years of my intense practice I used to wear kumkum on my fore head without fail. The desire was so much that even before going to bed in the night I used to wash my face and wear kumkum. (In Hindu religion wearing of kumkum on fore head by any male

is an indication that he is a spiritual person or
worshiping some God or at least he is a theist and
believes in Hindu philosophy).

After I stopped the intense meditation, the
desire to wear kumkum slowly disappeared.

The thinking

The spiritual knowledge I acquired, the peculiar understanding I gained is still with me. A different kind of 'looking at issues' developed in me. I started observing the ways of the world locally, nationally and internationally in all angles. Right from my college days, in more than three decades nearly, many changes have taken place at all spheres. I used to read the international news regularly. I feel that change in the political ideologies across the globe which affected millions of common people is a great concern. In these four decades there have been many social, cultural, political upheavals across the globe. The political upheavals resulted in disintegration of political identities and this resulted in untold human strife in some nations. Certain political ideologies were proved to be not-so-worthy because they failed on the economic front finally, and this resulted in suffering of the innocent common man. I feel very distressed on this front because though it is the common man who decides the course of human history, the common man is the least preferred subject.

I used to look with surprise at arms race of super powers in the seventies and eighties. There were strategic arms limitation treaties (SALT) between the super powers to limit the strategic arms. Every nation, small or big was pushed into some ideology group. Once there was a news item that the strategic arms might have been directed at New Delhi also. Another matter that evoked interest in me was Intercontinental Ballistic Missiles (ICBMs). These are otherwise the long distance computer aided detonator catapults of the mediaeval warfare! When will this human race stop the arms race? When will the life of common man be secure in spite of any wars between nations? When will the common man be free of juntas of some form or other around the world? When will these juntas get down safely the tigers they are riding and walk away without reprisals from the common man? Can there be a reconciliatory commission like ARC (African

Reconciliation Commission) everywhere, wherever there is a human conflict? It is accepted that the democracy is the best political system but will there be any democracy just as a model which will be free of fund collection mechanism which is the root cause of corruption and other evils in most of the democracies? Is there a new ideology in the offing in view of the changing scenario, because the mindset of the human race as on today is post industrial revolution of 16th century? Is there going to be a new revolution in the near future which will simply walk over the industrial revolution which occupies only one millionth part of the future human history? What happens to the values of today if a new revolution simply changes entire social, cultural, religious, political, economic and scientific scenarios across the globe?

Is the human simply an animal gifted with the thumb and not gifted with an intellect? If the human is really gifted with intellect, why are all these degradations in all spheres including environmental? When will the human treat the nature mother kindly?

When is the human going to be the citizen of the universe?

The man is not able to proudly declare that he is citizen of the world living with dignity. The man is still in search of his material existence only. When can he think of the non-matter for reaching the state of the eternal bliss? For this, man has to do a very long journey. This is beyond imagination of any intellectual on this planet earth. If this is the case, if there is any life force on some other planet in the universe, can the human race hold its head high in the universal community? If human race cannot set itself right, will this planet earth for its violations, be subjected to universal policing from other planets?

The solution

WE NEED NOT DO WILD IMAGINATIONS.

LET EVERYONE OF US MEDITATE FOR A
FRACTION OF A MINUTE.

*   *   *

What is the meaning of 'an individual becoming Antarmukh'?

As I had already told, our behavior is based on the values we set for ourselves and we also think that our personality is nothing but our behavior and our desires. However, an individual should identify himself as *'Chetana'* which is spread across this universe and which is beyond time, births and characteristics. He should be able to experience that *'Chetana'* within himself or feel the existence of the divinity within himself.

If an individual gets such experience, his mind becomes very light. Tranquility rests in his mind.

It comes to his understanding as to how far the running race that he is taking up in his life is meaningful and how far it is relevant.

Simultaneously, if an individual does not have inclination to discharge his duties or responsibilities, it comes to his understanding as to how far his disinclination to discharge duties or responsibilities is relevant.

Meaning of 'becoming *Antarmukh*' is becoming ready in life with the understanding of the above.

What is the method of becoming 'Antarmukh'?

This is a kind of meditation.

The individual should close his eyes and be able to bring into his consciousness calmly the '*Chetana*' which is spread across this universe.

He should experience this calmness within himself fully.

Another important matter is that people think that meditation is a process of concentration in a seated posture. Generally people think that they have to reach the state of concentration in postures of Padmasana or Vajrasana. For doing meditation in such postures, in fact, many people do not have the habit of sitting in these postures.

If *Dhyana* (meditation) is practiced in these postures, before reaching the state of meditation, legs become numb or the individual has to adjust himself in the seated position again to continue that posture. Hence in this *Antarmukhi Dhyana*, the individual can lie on a flat surface or floor facing the sky, placing his left leg on his right leg and keeping both the hands in the place between his heart and navel. Closing eyes, the individual can enter the state of *Dhyana*.

One can also do *Dhyana* in seated posture if one feels it convenient. The result will be the same.

After getting into meditation

First, when we close our eyes, different persons appear in our mind. Different contexts come to our remembrance. Like this, different pictures will be moving on our mind screen. We try to stop these thoughts by observing them closely. We will be trying to reach certain state of concentration about which we do not know clearly.

In this book I have been repeating different thoughts and ideas because before entering the process of *Dhyana*, we should have specific idea about ourselves. This repetition of thoughts is for forming an opinion about ourselves and our position in this universe.

Now I tell you how to enter the meditation or *Dhyana*. This is an imaginary state. First of all, we should take ourselves out of the present situations and circumstances.

How then?

First, we should psychologically travel above this earth. To where we are traveling is the place where the God exists, to see the God and that too with the belief that His association is answer to all.

When we are traveling above, i.e., into the space, first we go above the place where we are. If we travel further above, we will go above the area where we stay. Next we will go above the country where we stay. Now we are in the sky and we can see the places, areas, and the country far below. If we travel further above, we are able to see the planet earth fully from the space. From there we can see at distance, rivers, mountains, cities, forests and oceans. If we travel further above, we go above the atmosphere of the earth. If we travel further above, we will enter the solar system by crossing the orbit of this earth. Once we cross this orbit of the earth, there will be neither day nor night. There will be light everywhere. If we stand in between the planets of this solar system, we will see the planets revolving round the Sun. The earth will also be rotating and be slowly moving.

If we travel out of this solar system, if we go farther and farther, it will be surprising if we see on our mind screen, the solar system which is very far.

We have taken birth on the planet earth of the solar system which is very far from us. There we have formed our bondages and we are living as per the traditions and customs being followed there. We are bound to the thoughts and values of that planet earth. Our aspirations, excitements, disappointments, disheartening experiences, victories, failures, fears, dishonors, respects and recognitions and even the insults are related to the happenings on this planet earth only.

Now where are we?
If we move farther and farther and away?
If we have only a soul that can think, without a
physical body?

And the destination which we are traveling to is to see certain divine power which is beyond all the million billion trillion stars, beyond innumerable solar systems and to see certain divine power which is holding all these together.

After traveling some more distance, we see at a distance, a great stream of light flowing down from sky. With great surprise, we travel towards that stream of light. There is a large golden canopy with glow of diamonds, with high pillars of gold studded with precious stones of different colors. On other side of this large golden canopy, our beloved Lord is seated in a dazzling, high throne of gold studded with diamonds and precious stones of different colors. He is the Lord of this universe. He is the representative of the Universal Consciousness or the 'Chetana' which is spread across this universe. He is a mine of knowledge. He is replica of all noble qualities. He is himself the light and glow. He is too beautiful. This entire universe is moving at his graceful looks. His power is reflecting in this entire universe. On our nearing that large, wonderful golden canopy, the Lord of light and glow, smiled at us passing looks of grace towards us. We remained there looking at the shape of the Lord with our wide open eyes, with our body trembling.

Behold! In that large canopy there are hundreds of persons who are with great joy, enjoying the loving and graceful looks of the Lord. Some are singing in praise of the Lord. Some are discussing among themselves, looking at the Lord immersed in joy, about the magnanimity of that powerful Lord. We will be astonished if we know who these persons are.

They are those prophets, men of knowledge, seekers of truth, visionaries, great yogis and saints and great personalities, who, since the onset of this mankind which is blessed with the power of thinking, had taken births on this earth in different times, in different circumstances, in different places, holding the torch, showed the path of the light to the human race, withstanding all sufferings of body, sufferings in this worldly affairs and also withstanding many dishonors and rather insults on earth. It is they who are praising the Lord immersed in joy. In the proximity of the Lord they do not have any sufferings. They do not have any fears. All their aspirations are fulfilled. They do not have any ambitions. They need not impress anybody. They are above all values. To all these great people, with great respect, let us bow one thousand million times.

Now we are at this great, dazzling, colorful canopy of our Lord. Let us bow to the Lord of this universe once.

Let us also request our Lord: "Oh! Lord, take me near to you. Take me away from all these dualities. Keep me away from all that is false and keep me near truth"

Let us again request Lord to forgive our mistakes. Let us agree in His presence that there is nothing which is more than his grace. Let us request our Lord to bestow full happiness and prosperity to this world.

In this state, let us remain for one minute, two minutes, five minutes, ten minutes, fifteen minutes or any more time that we wish.

If we are in His proximity, no one can do anything to us. His proximity is itself a great ring of power and safety. At his wink anything can happen.

Spending like this for some time, let us come down, bowing to Him obediently once again.

—Enjoy this peaceful state of meditation.
Enjoy peace.—

*   *   *

We become 'Antarmukh': when and where?

The surprise here is, to whatever may be the farther ends of this unending universe that we may travel, is it not that we travel within ourselves? It means that we have extended ourselves to the imaginary flow of power. We have not only seen the universe within us, but we have also seen ourselves within us.

Breathing methods and meditation

What I think is, for breathing methods and breathing techniques the center point is 'body and mind' whereas for meditation, the center point is 'feelings about soul and the Supreme Soul'.

In the method of meditation which I mentioned, regulation of breathing happens without our effort for that. We need not show special attention for breathing. But in this method of meditation breathing activity runs healthily and improves health.

One important point is, breathing or regulation of breathing cannot be meditation. Similarly meditation may be useful as a relaxation technique, but no relaxation technique can be meditation.

Here I want to specially stress something about breathing techniques and its relation to meditation:

In fact this is a matter of controversy.

In ancient times in India there was a sage. In his name, there is a treatise. The sage in his treatise refers many interesting topics including supernatural powers a person who does spiritual practice can attain.

He starts his treatise with eight basic tenets for any spiritual practitioner:

These may be listed, in simple and general terms as follows:

1) Moral codes and discipline in the external world
2) Internal purification of the mind and soul
3) Posture for doing meditation
4) Breath Control
5) Control of senses
6) Attaining concentration

7) Meditation
8) Absorption of the self in to the Universal Consciousness

You might have observed that out of these eight tenets or rather stages in spiritual practice, meditation is a state just before absorption of the self into the Universal Consciousness.

Out of the above eight steps, 4th, 5th and 6th stages can be attained by getting into the stage of meditation directly because you will enter stages of breath control, sense control and a stage of concentration automatically. For this you may try it.

While it is a fact that meditation leads to a kind of breath control, and there is a link between breathing and meditation, it is not correct to assert that without breath control one cannot attain concentration.

Now as on today in many meditation or yoga centers meditation or rather philosophical thinking starts with breathing techniques.

In my experience, I understood that the spiritual practitioners are not in a position to attain further stage after practicing the breathing techniques. Interestingly I came across a spiritual practitioner who was taught well in breathing methods in a yoga and philosophy center. He questioned me, 'what else will any spiritual practitioner do otherwise, than concentrating on breathing when he sits for meditation?'

I had an interesting interaction with another spiritual practitioner once. He was rather unhappy because he could not attain further stage of spiritual realization what saints professed, after following breathing techniques. I felt awful when he expressed that he had great difficulty in coming out of the compulsion of doing the breathing exercises daily, as otherwise he used to feel uneasy throughout the day because of not practicing of breathing exercise. He expressed that he joined a meditation center out of the desire to see the state of the eternal bliss with a full philosophical mood and ultimately he ended up in practicing breathing techniques as a compulsion and with great difficulty he got rid of this habit.

I had also come across a spiritual practitioner who did meditation, when surrounded in a busy crowd. He was invited to deliver a lecture on spirituality in a town where I was in that town on my job. This spiritual practitioner belonged to certain system of philosophy. Before going to the dais to deliver the lecture he meditated for about 10 to 15 seconds sitting in the chair there itself. I clearly observed him when he got into the mood of meditation without even closing his eyes, in that busy crowd.

Meditation is a spark, not a process

Some persons question me about the time I spend daily in meditation.

When I answer to them that meditation is a spark and not a process they will be puzzled.

The answer is like this because when meditation undergoes a breathing process, certain amount of time is involved in inhalation, retention and exhalation.

Besides the eight stages mentioned by a sage in ancient India as I said in the earlier pages, I also believe that a spiritual practitioner may directly start doing meditation and this be the case I say that there are only three stages to reach the state of the eternal bliss or absorption of the self into the Universal Consciousness.

1) Meditation
2) True knowledge
3) Absorption of the self into the Universal Consciousness.

I believe in the above three stages because it is the true knowledge that takes an individual to the state of the eternal bliss or absorption of the self into the Universal Consciousness.

I further believe that in the history of the mankind, the prophets, and great saints and other great personalities had in fact only two stages in their spiritual lives. These two stages are the true knowledge and absorption of the self into the Universal Consciousness. And I also believe that these great souls, or otherwise to be called 'representatives of God' were in fact part of the Universal Consciousness, with only difference being that each one of them was wearing a physical body like us.

Or otherwise we can also say that their souls were wearing physical bodies!

With this we can also conclude that they were always in the stage of meditation and they were permanently living with the divine spark till they left their physical bodies. I also conclude that their lives themselves are sparks. When they tried to explain to us the Universal Logic which they visualized, to the humanity, some of those great souls were not received by the humanity properly.

Speech—thought—experience

Mind can think, come to conclusions in different angles. Our mind deceives us by forcing us to conclude basing on what we see, listen, read or understand. One can speak at length through mind basing on what one sees, listens, reads or understands. One can gain great 'spiritual knowledge' through these. But without going deep into the mind, without undergoing spiritual experiences through self-practice the 'spiritual knowledge' gained will not be of much use.

I wish to say like this: 'Behind the 'waterfall' of speech there is 'waterfall' of thoughts and behind 'waterfall' of thoughts there is an unlimited volume of water which is still and deep'

Meditation takes us to that still and deep water, and we can call it elixir, the sea of tranquility, which is the sea of knowledge and this knowledge is gained by the spiritual experience or the self-realization.

What is the ideal place for meditation?

If we do meditation directly under the blue sky the result will be incomparable. This means there should not be any shade between us and the sky. Similarly meditation in the moonlight will be wonderful.

In fact, meditation may be done in any place that is comfortable to you. You may sit in your room on the floor and do your meditation. You can sit in your chair and do your meditation in your place. You can even stand and do your meditation for a moment. Only concern is that you may lose your balance and fall when you are in a standing position. Even in the standing position, in a moment, you can take your mind to the farther ends of this universe, see God and again come back. This meditation for one moment gives you great strength. You can practically experience this.

You may go to garden or to some open place and do meditation in fresh air.

Sitting or standing or lying in an erect and stretched position of the body may be the requisite because your concentration in the meditation may prompt you to have a free and deep breath.

Arguments on matters of spirituality

One more important matter I want to tell is, please do not discuss with others about the feelings you have after you get into meditation. Do not argue. Do not try to convince someone.

We should remember one important point. The meditation that does not improve our mental happiness and our human relations is a mere waste. You should feel fortunate if you get great feelings.

Please spend your time reading good books and scriptures. Compare your wonderful feelings with those mentioned in scriptures and good books and feel inner happiness.

There are many good books and scriptures which tell about the pure Supreme Soul and its greatness. There are good books in every religion.

The ultimate guide that leads you to right conclusion is your spiritual practice only. Correct yardstick to measure purity of your thoughts is your pure spirituality only.

Meditation is a practice, quest and an interesting journey day by day

Many people think that meditation is a method of concentration and a practice to reach God. But with what we can compare this is, imagine that we have climbed a beautiful and wonderful mountain. We will find a more beautiful and wonderful mountain at a distance.

Similarly, imagine that we entered a cave, which is beautiful and wonderful. Enjoying the beauties of this cave, on reaching the end of this cave, we will find beginning of another cave with a great light. We will continue our journey. We continue getting such thrilling experiences. Every experience will take us to a new identity. We will be nearing to see our own self. Because of the divine feelings, we will perceive at all things as equal and the feeling of fulfillment will change our overall view towards this external world. The feelings of discontentment and disheartening will vanish. The strength of the divine will accompany our strength. We will have great self-confidence. Inferiority complex within us will go away.

In this journey of mediation, by the time we are nearing our destination, the impressions made within us by ourselves will also change.

Meditation is a spiritual journey: up to where?

This spiritual journey will come to
an end when an individual:

*** FINDS HIMSELF ***
*** FINDS GOD ***
AND
*** FINDS THAT BOTH ARE SAME ***

*   *   *